MARIAN CONSECRATION
for Families with Young Children

Colleen Pressprich

Our Sunday Visitor
Huntington, Indiana

Nihil Obstat
Msgr. Michael Heintz, Ph.D.
Censor Librorum

Imprimatur
✠ Kevin C. Rhoades
Bishop of Fort Wayne-South Bend
June 3, 2020

The *Nihil Obstat* and Imprimatur are official declarations that a book is free from doctrinal or moral error. It is not implied that those who have granted the *Nihil Obstat* and *Imprimatur* agree with the contents, opinions, or statements expressed.

Except where noted, the Scripture citations used in this work are taken from the *Revised Standard Version of the Bible — Second Catholic Edition* (Ignatius Edition), copyright © 1965, 1966, 2006 National Council of the Churches of Christ in the United States of America. Used by permission. All rights reserved.

Every reasonable effort has been made to determine copyright holders of excerpted materials and to secure permissions as needed. If any copyrighted materials have been inadvertently used in this work without proper credit being given in one form or another, please notify Our Sunday Visitor in writing so that future printings of this work may be corrected accordingly.

Our Sunday Visitor Publishing Division
Our Sunday Visitor, Inc.
200 Noll Plaza
Huntington, IN 46750
1-800-348-2440

ISBN: 978-1-68192-490-8 (Inventory No. T2380)
1. JUVENILE NONFICTION—Religion—Devotional & Prayer.
2. JUVENILE NONFICTION—Religion—Christianity—Christian Life.
3. RELIGION—Christianity—Catholic.

LCCN: 2020937003

Cover design: Amanda Falk
Cover art: Rebecca Górzyńska; AdobeStock
Interior design: Amanda Falk
Interior art: Rebecca Górzyńska; AdobeStock

PRINTED IN THE UNITED STATES OF AMERICA

For my children, who have taught and inspired me ever since they were born. — C. P.

For Emilka, Maksio, Tadzio, and Leon. — R. G.

TABLE OF CONTENTS

Author's Note

I made my first consecration to Mary in college. Now, over a decade later, I eagerly look forward every year to renewing my consecration on the feast of the Immaculate Conception. The thirty-three-day preparation period has become a time of grace and growth for me, a time to recenter my life on the Lord and delve deeper into that relationship, despite the challenges of this season of raising young children.

But what a gift those children have been for my faith, and what a gift to watch them grow in theirs! I was not raised in a practicing Catholic family myself (my parents were Easter and Christmas Catholics, though they did dutifully send my brother and me to Catechism class each week), so I never experienced Catholicism on a daily basis as a child. Our eldest daughter, Gianna, soaks up everything we read or show her. Through her, I've realized how natural faith is to a little one. I see in her life the truth that baptism does remove the stain of original sin and that even though we have a fallen nature, we were created to turn toward the Lord.

This year, as my anniversary of consecration approached, I began to think about ways to invite Gianna into this important aspect of my own faith life. I searched for Marian Consecrations for children, and while I found some beautiful ones designed for older children and teens, there were none written with a preschooler in mind. So, at the urging of my husband, I started to write, thinking all the time of my daughter and what I wanted to share with her about Mary and Jesus. I'm so excited to be able to share these reflections with your children as well.

This consecration preparation is designed to be done together with your child and be an interactive experience. It is purposefully designed to leave space for each parent to answer questions that may arise and share his or her own experiences of devotion to Our Lady. If your own devotion to Mary is just beginning, that's okay! I hope that this preparation allows you and your child to grow in love of Our Blessed Mother together. The meditation for each day is followed by a few conversation starters. These are meant to be a jumping-off point for faith-filled dialogue.

I hope that this consecration preparation will help your family to build your little domestic church the way it has ours.
With prayers,
Colleen Pressprich

Getting Started

Dear Parents,

I realize that it can be daunting to think about completing a consecration to Mary at all, much less one that involves small, wriggling children with short attention spans. I wanted to share some of what our family does in the hope of encouraging and empowering you.

Consecrating your family to Jesus through Mary is a powerful experience; I would even say a life-changing one. To be consecrated means to be set apart for a sacred purpose, and by consecrating ourselves to Mary we put our lives in her hands, asking for her help to become more devoted to her Son, Jesus. It helps us grow in holiness and increase in faith, hope, and love.

You'll notice that the preparation period is thirty-three days long. This is based on Saint Louis de Montfort's Consecration to Jesus through Mary. In his book, *True Devotion to Mary*, Saint Louis lays out a thirty-three-day course that is designed to help free us from our attachments to the world as well as learn more about ourselves, Jesus, and Mary. In writing this book, I wanted to keep the spirit of his model, while making it accessible for families and little ones.

ESTABLISH A RITUAL

Rituals are something that the Catholic Church is great at. We absolutely rock at rituals. In a time when new and different is often pitched as better, we Catholics love to sink down deeply into the comfort of knowing what to expect. I can be certain that my pastor is going to be wearing green on any Sunday of Ordinary Time. I know that the smell of incense means we are celebrating a high feast. I can recognize as friends and familiar faces the saints in stained glass at churches around the world, because they are always depicted with the same signs — Saint Joseph holds a lily; Saint Peter, keys. Saint Clare carries a monstrance, while a wolf stands next to Saint Francis. Even more so than for adults, rituals are very helpful for children. The routine of rituals helps your children to feel comfortable, which opens up their minds to learning new information and thinking in different ways.

Home rituals don't have to be extensive, and they don't have to be complicated. In fact, simple is better with young children, and in my experience, have also often proved to be the most profound. For example, in our house, when we begin our classroom time (as we call homeschooling work), we all kneel down together in the center of our classroom and pray these simple words:

"Thank you, dear Lord, for this precious new day. Please guide us in love as we grow, work, and play." That's it, the entirety of our morning offering. It takes only a moment, but it is reverent, and it has become a habit. On the occasional morning that I forget, one of the kids is quick to remind me that we haven't done it. It helps all of us, me included, to remember to center our day on the Lord.

For us, establishing a ritual has been crucial to helping parts of our faith to stick with our kids. My *Marian Consecration for Families with Young Children* is designed with ritual in mind. I suggest that each day you begin with an Our Father and end with a Hail Mary. The simple rhythm of each day's prayers will help your children feel comfortable and settle into the routine of praying. Beginning and ending with the same prayers will help your children to relax and to enter into the meditations in a deeper way because they will know what to expect.

Similarly, we have found that choosing a consistent location has been a key component in establishing rituals in our family. This past year, for our Marian Consecration, Gianna and I always read the meditation together snuggled up in the "big bed" (mom and dad's bed). The big bed is a special location in our family. Being there makes the children feel safe. It is a place for snuggles and comfort and peace. I encourage you to think about where that place is in your home. Where do you read bedtime stories? Where do you cuddle the child who has a scraped knee? Where is your family's safe space? Choosing the right location helps set the tone for prayer time. My advice is to choose somewhere cozy.

BE FLEXIBLE

This may seem like a strange piece of advice following a discussion on the importance of ritual, but they aren't mutually exclusive. Rituals are important, but flexibility is key in actually managing to live them out when young kids are involved. I have found with my own kids that the more rigid I try to be with making sure that everything happens at exactly the right time in exactly the right way, the more the kids push against it. In our home, it has worked well to establish set times of prayer in our house that are built around activities and not times. For example, we pray before we begin schoolwork, before we eat, before bed. The hours of those times of day might fluctuate, but because the prayer is tied to the activity it doesn't get lost in the shuffle. This allows our day to flow more naturally. For this consecration, I would suggest finding a pocket of time either before or after an activity in your house that occurs daily, and try to add the preparation in there.

I say "try," because some days everything falls apart. Someone gets sick, or misses a much-needed nap, or dinner burns, or traffic keeps you or your spouse from getting home on time, or any of a million complications that are a part of family life. This consecration is written as a thirty-three-day preparation, but those days do not have to be consecutive. Maybe your family can do one meditation together a week on a Sunday. Maybe you try your best and manage five days a week and not the other two. That is okay. That is better than okay. The purpose of this book is to bring you and your children closer to Mary, Jesus, and each other, not to make you feel guilty for being imperfect.

Take as long as you need or want to finish based on your family's schedule and needs. Make your own calendar for completion. Take it slow or speed it up — whatever is best for you and your family. Mary will certainly not mind if your family consecrates itself to her on a regular old day of the week! If you want to aim for a particular feast day, though, you'll find a short calendar at the end of the section For Parents.

MAKE IT SPECIAL

No matter when your consecration date is, make a big deal of it. A consecration is a tremendous, life-changing thing. And while your children won't fully understand the depth and gravity of it, you can help them by putting it into perspective. Think about the important days they have experienced already — birthdays, holidays, feast days. What do those look like in your family? What outward signs make them special?

Plan a celebration for your family that will help your children understand that Consecration Day is a special day too. If special events in your family involve extended family, consider inviting grandparents or aunts and uncles to attend Mass with you. If your family culture involves a lot of food, cook a special dish together or go out to eat. Maybe your children love balloons as much as mine do, and the mark of an event's specialness is whether or not there will be balloons.

Regardless of what else you do to make the day stand out, definitely attend Mass together as a family. When we complete our consecration, at the end of Mass, we wait until the church is quiet, and then make our way to the side altar dedicated to Our Lady. And kneeling before her, we quietly recite together (I have them say the words after me) a simple prayer of consecration. Then we end with a Hail Mary.

FOLLOW THE CHILD

Each day of the consecration preparation includes some conversation starters to facilitate discussion with your child about the day's topic. The questions are those that I have found fruitful to ask my own children, that have sparked their imagination, and helped further their understanding of doctrine.

Each set of questions is just a suggestion. Please don't feel as though you have to get through all of them in order to check off your work for the day. With an exercise like this I try to apply as much as possible Maria Montessori's principle of "following the child." This means that I may ask a question and find that my child has a great deal to say on the subject, or many questions about it, that will naturally suggest different follow-ups than I had planned. Allow the conversation with your children to flow naturally and follow where they lead.

On the other side of the equation, you may find that when you ask a question, your children might not have anything to say. That is okay. It very well may be that they need to think more about it, to process the information more slowly, and hours or days later they will surprise you with a comment on the topic. This is often the case with our middle child. William is a deep thinker, but not a quick one. He, like his dad, prefers to process internally, make sure he has his thoughts in order, and only then, share them. His older sister is the opposite — she thinks quickly and processes verbally.

Keep in mind that you don't have to use these conversation starters right after you read the day's meditations. If your child's attention span has waned, consider coming back to them at another point in the day. Something that has helped our family have conversations that feel much more natural (as opposed to an interrogation) has been to find an activity that we can do together while we talk. Some of our deepest conversations with our children have been while we have colored alongside them. Sometimes we each have our own coloring sheet, sometimes we collaborate on the same page. But as we sit next to our children and share an experience, we've found it easier to share our hearts with them. Gianna particularly enjoys chatting over a box of colored pencils. It's one of my favorite ways of engaging her. But even quiet, pondering William opens up over a coloring book.

Your family's favorite activity might be something completely different. Perhaps you like to hike together and can use the opportunity of being outside in God's beautiful creation to turn the conversation to faith. Maybe your child really likes to build with blocks, and over a carefully constructed city you can segue a conversation from architecture to the building blocks of faith.

The conversation starters are also there to offer tips for sharing your own faith journey with your children. When I was a missionary with Life Teen, we had a saying: "You have to earn the right to be heard." We recognized that we couldn't expect to preach faith and obedience to the rules of the Church to teens if we hadn't first built a relationship with them. I have found that the same is true with my children. If my husband and I want our children to see that the faith we want to pass down to them is worthwhile, we can't just talk the talk, we have to walk the walk. It will be a hard sell for them to embrace Catholicism, and specifically a deep relationship with Our Lady, if we haven't convinced them with our lives. Pope Paul VI wrote in *Evangelii Nuntiandi* that "more trust is placed in witnesses than in teachers." As parents, we are called to be both to our children.

This mission can be overwhelming at times. But we cannot allow ourselves to be paralyzed by the greatness of the task set before us. We must put our hand to the plow and go. That's what the conversation starters for each day are designed to help you do. They are also questions designed to help you gain insight into your child's precious soul. You'll find more tips and insights in the parent section in the back of the book. I suggest you read each day's note for parents before beginning the reflection with your child each day.

What Is a Marian Consecration?

To consecrate something means to dedicate it, to set it apart for a special purpose. When we make a consecration to Mary, we are giving ourselves to her care, putting ourselves in her hands, so that she can bring us to Jesus. And Mary **always** brings us to Jesus. This is a very big, important decision. For the rest of your life, you will be hers, and she will love and take care of you always, and guide you to love Jesus more. Your relationship with Mary will be special, and you will trust her with your life, your needs, and your wants.

WHY DO WE PREPARE FOR OUR CONSECRATION?

Because this is such an important moment, we spend time preparing ourselves for it. We will spend thirty-three days reading and praying together to get our hearts ready for Mary. We will get to know who she is and what the Bible says about her. We will ponder some of the things we can learn from Mary's example, and we will learn about a few of the times that she has appeared to people and given them a special message to share with the world. We will also learn some of the Church's prayers to Mary.

This is time we will spend together, learning and growing in faith. It will be a time for snuggles and conversation, for prayers and questions. Every day, we will begin with the Sign of the Cross and say the Our Father. After we have read and prayed, we will end with a Hail Mary. Let's begin this journey together!

Day One

Mary Was a Little Girl Once

Mary was a little girl once. She grew up in Nazareth, a town in Galilee, over 2,000 years ago. Mary lived with her mom and dad, Saints Anne and Joachim, who were Jesus' grandparents. Her mom and dad taught her to love God, just like your parents do. We don't know very much about what Mary's childhood was like, but there are some Catholic traditions (things that the Church has taught and believed for hundreds of years) that give us clues.

Mary was Jewish. That means she was one of God's chosen people, the Israelites that we read about in the Old Testament. When she only three years old, Mary went to the Temple in Jerusalem to learn about God and be dedicated to him. When we say she was "dedicated," we mean that Mary belonged to God completely! She loved him and wanted to do his will even from her childhood.

We celebrate Mary's birthday on September 8 every year. We also celebrate the day she was presented to God at the temple in Jerusalem, on November 21.

Conversation Starters _____

- Do you think that Mary had a favorite game or toy when she was a little girl?
- What do you think her favorite food was?
- Do you think Mary had chores to do as a girl?

- What questions do you have about Mary as a child?
- What do you think Saint Anne and Mary are talking about in this picture?

Day Two

Mary Is the Immaculate Conception

When Adam and Eve decided to eat the forbidden fruit, they sinned against God. They did not trust that he loved them and wanted what was best for them. This first sin was what we call the *original sin*. Because of their sin, Adam and Eve lost God's grace and were cast out of the garden. Every person born since then has been born without God's grace filling us. Because of original sin, it is easier for us to choose the wrong thing and harder for us to choose God.

When God decided to send his Son into the world as a baby, he knew that he needed someone free from sin to help him. God created Mary without original sin, so that she would be filled with grace and able to be the perfect mother for Jesus. We call this the Immaculate Conception, and it's one of our special names for Mary. *Immaculate* means perfectly clean. *Conception* is the moment a baby is created in her mother's womb. So when we say that Mary is the Immaculate Conception, we are saying that she was created perfectly clean and full of grace in her mom's belly.

Mary never sinned, and never chose to do anything that would take her away from God. Sin always hurts our relationship with God and with other people. When we feel tempted to do something wrong, we can ask Mary to pray for us and help us to be strong.

Conversation Starters

- What questions do you have about original sin?
- What questions do you have about what it means that Mary is the Immaculate Conception?
- What do you think are some things you and I can do to avoid doing things that we know aren't good for us?

- What do you notice in this illustration? Can you find any of the hidden pictures in the tree behind Saint Anne and Mary? What do you think they mean?

Day Three

Prayer to the Immaculate Conception

Yesterday, we learned that Mary is the Immaculate Conception. Today, let's learn one of the Church's prayers about this title of Mary. Pay attention to what this prayer asks God. At the end of the prayer we'll talk about what it means. We can say it as many times as you'd like.

> Father, the image of the Virgin is found in the Church. Mary had a faith that your Spirit prepared and a love that never knew sin, for you kept her sinless from the first moment of her conception. Trace in our actions the lines of her love, in our hearts her readiness of faith. Prepare once again a world for your Son who lives and reigns with you and the Holy Spirit, one God, forever and ever. Amen.[1]

This prayer talks about tracing the lines of Mary's love; when we trace, we follow a path that's already there. Just like it's easier to trace your hand, than to draw a picture of it, we will find it easier to love if we follow Mary's path! That's one of the reasons we're learning about her.

Conversation Starters

- Have you ever done any tracing? Was it easier or harder for you to draw a picture of the thing you traced?

- What do you think it means for God to trace Mary's love in our hearts?
- Look at Mary in this picture. What do you think she's thinking about?

---

1. *Catholic Household Blessings and Prayers*, United States Conference of Catholic Bishops (Washington, D.C.: USCCB Publishing, 1989), 14.

Day Four

Mary Is the Mother of God

Another name we use for Mary is *Theotokos*. This is a Greek word, and it means "God-bearer." It means she carried God in her womb, that she was the Mother of God. When Mary said yes to becoming the mother of Jesus, she said yes to being the Mother of God, because Jesus is God the Son.

Think about how you feel about your mom. Do you love her? Do you like to hug and snuggle her? Does she take care of you? Does she play with you and love spending time with you? It was just like that with Jesus and Mary. When Jesus was a baby, Mary nursed him, carried him, and changed his diapers. She comforted him and kissed him when he got hurt. As he grew up, Mary taught him, loved him, played with him, and kept him safe. She was always there for him.

Mary loved Jesus unconditionally. That means she loved him no matter what, and would always support him. And in return, Jesus loved Mary just like you love your mom. He obeyed her and listened to her, and loved to be near her. He talked with her and played with her. She was his mommy.

Conversation Starters

- What do you think was Jesus' favorite activity to do with Mary?
- What do you think Mary liked to do with Jesus when he was young?

- How does it make you feel when you think about Mary snuggling Jesus? What do you think Mary was thinking about when she was snuggling and nursing him like the illustration shows?

Day Five

Mary Is Our Mom Too

When Jesus was on the cross, his mom was there with him. Mary stood on the ground next to him, and it helped him to have her nearby while he was in pain (just like it helps you to have your mom close when you get hurt). He knew that soon he would die, and that after rising from the dead, he would go back to heaven. That meant Jesus would have to leave his mom for awhile. He didn't want her to be all alone, so he spoke to his disciple, John, who was also standing next to the cross. He knew that he could trust John, because John loved Jesus very much. Jesus told John that Mary would be John's mother from now on, and he told Mary to think of John as a son. John brought Mary to his house and took care of her for the rest of her life on earth. In return, Mary took care of John too. She prayed for him and helped him to know God better. She loved him very much, and he became her child.

But here's something special — we believe that when Jesus was saying to John, "Behold, your mother," he was also talking to all of us. Jesus knew that just like John, we would need Mary as our mother. And she loves us just like she loves Jesus. If we run to her in prayer when we are hurt or scared or upset, she will comfort us and ask Jesus to help us. She loves it when we tell her all about our days, the fun we had, the things that challenged us. We can talk to her just like we talk to our mommies.

Conversation Starters

- What are some things that you would like to tell Mary about your day today?
- Would you like to talk with her now together?
- Are there any times you have felt that Mary has helped you?

Day Six

The Memorare

Yesterday we learned that Mary is our mother. Today, let's pray a special prayer to her. It's called the Memorare. This prayer asks Mary as our mom to help us when we are in need, and in it we run to her side, just like you run to your mother when you need help.

Remember, O most gracious Virgin Mary, that never was it known that anyone who fled to thy protection, implored thy help, or sought thine intercession was left unaided. Inspired by this confidence, I fly unto thee, O Virgin of virgins, my mother; to thee do I come, before thee I stand, sinful and sorrowful. O Mother of the Word Incarnate, despise not my petitions, but in thy mercy hear and answer me. Amen.

Conversation Starters _____

- Were there any words in the Memorare prayer that you didn't know? Can I explain them to you?

- Do you have anything you want to ask Mary's help with?

Day Seven

Mary Is Filled with the Holy Spirit

The Holy Spirit is the third Person of the Trinity. When Mary said yes to God and agreed to be Jesus' mom, she was filled with the Holy Spirit. We say that the Spirit of God *overshadowed* her. That means that God covered her and surrounded her, like when you're in a plane and suddenly the clouds are all around you and they're all you can see.

We sometimes call Mary the *spouse* or wife of the Holy Spirit because the Holy Spirit was so close to her. Because she was so filled with the Holy Spirit, Mary was able to hear God and love God well, better than any other person on earth. She was there at Pentecost, when the Holy Spirit came down on the apostles. She helped them to not be afraid and encouraged them. We can ask the Holy Spirit to be in us too, and Mary will help us to do that. By getting to know Mary, we get to know the Holy Spirit.

Conversation Starters

- What do you know about the Holy Spirit?
- What questions do you have about the Holy Spirit?
- Besides the story of Pentecost, can you think of other places in the Bible where we hear about the Holy Spirit?
- How does he help us?

Day Eight

Mary Is Queen of Heaven

When Mary was assumed into heaven (when we talk about Mary's *assumption*, we mean that God took her body to heaven when he took her soul), God crowned her the Queen of Heaven. What does that mean? Being a queen is a very high honor. Queens here on earth are in charge. They rule, and they are powerful.

As Queen of Heaven, Mary is also powerful. She is queen because her Son is King, but also because she helped Jesus to save us by agreeing to be his mom. Jesus lets Mary give graces to us, and lets her help answer our prayers, because she is Queen of Heaven. He listens to her and loves her, and she cooperates with him in heaven just like she did here on earth.

Conversation Starters

- What do you think it felt like for Mary to see Jesus again?
- What do you think it was like in heaven when Mary was crowned queen?

- Jesus and Mary look so happy to see each other in this illustration. Can you imagine what Jesus is saying to her? What do you think Mary said to Jesus when she saw him again?

Day Nine

Mary Always Leads Us to Jesus

Saint Louis de Montfort, a man who loved Mary very much, said, "Mary is the safest, easiest, shortest, and most perfect way of approaching Jesus." He reminds us that Mary always leads us to Jesus. When we ask Mary for help, she calls to Jesus and brings him with her to aid us.

Everything that Mary does, she does because she loves Jesus and wants to do his will. She wants what Jesus wants and tries to help us want it too. Mary knows that we will be fulfilled and joyful when we are with God and doing his will. She wants the best for us, and the best is to know and love Jesus.

Conversation Starters

- What are some of the ways Mary leads people to Jesus?
- Are there any people you would like to ask Mary to bring to her Son?

- What do you notice about this illustration? How does it make you feel?

Day Ten

How to Say Yes to God

Sometimes saying yes to what God wants for us is hard to do, just like sometimes it's hard to obey your parents. But just like your parents, God only wants good things for your life. Sometimes we don't understand all of God's commandments (which are God's rules and help us get to heaven). When you were a toddler, you didn't understand all of mom and dad's rules, like why you had to wear a coat in the winter. Sometimes a toddler wants to go outside without a jacket, and his mom or dad will make him wear one because they know he will be cold. It's like that with God too.

Mary always said yes to God. When the angel Gabriel came to her and asked her to be the mother of Jesus, she said, "Behold, I am the handmaid of the Lord; let it be to me according to your word." She didn't understand how she would have a baby or how that baby would be the Son of God, but she trusted God's plan. Her mom and dad raised to her to know God, so she knew that he was good and only wanted good things for his people. Even when she saw Jesus being crucified, she still trusted that God had a plan. She can help us to love and follow God even when bad things happen to us, when we feel frustrated or angry, or when we don't understand.

Conversation Starters

- Can you think of any time when it was hard for you to say yes to your parents, but later you were happy you did?
- Do you think Mary ever had a hard time saying yes to God? What do you think helped her during those moments?

- What do you think is happening in this illustration? What might Mary be thinking about here? How does this picture make you feel?

Day Eleven

How to Be in the Presence of God

Mary got to live with Jesus. She got to hug him and hold him and hear him laugh and talk. What a blessing! Jesus was her child, so she was always in the presence of God when she was with him. Even after Jesus went back to heaven, she prayed to him and kept his words and his will in her heart. And she could receive him in the Eucharist. Jesus gave Mary ways to keep him with her, and he gives them to us too.

We can't see God the way that Mary did, so sometimes it can be hard to remember that he is always there with us. But we can learn how to talk to him and share with him the way that Mary did. We can stop for quick moments throughout our day to ask Jesus to join us and be with us as we play, when we learn, as we eat, before we go to sleep. Jesus loves to be with us and loves to be invited into our lives. He will be so excited to be a part of your day,

We can also be with Jesus when we go to Mass or to adoration. He is present in the Eucharist, there with us, and when we are old enough, we can receive him into our bodies. It's important to take time to pay attention during Mass, to pray and to offer thanks to Jesus for all the gifts he has given you.

Conversation Starters

- What are some ways that we can work together to remember that Jesus is with us throughout our day?

Day Twelve

Meekness

Meek is a word often used to describe Mary.

Meekness can be best understood as having strength that is under control. People who are meek are patient and calm when difficult things happen. They choose to be prayerful and trust in God rather than lash out in anger. They make the choice to be prayerful and trust in God. They have learned when they should use their strength and when they should not.

Think about how strong and brave Mary was. She took a long journey to visit and take care of her cousin Elizabeth. She traveled to Egypt, far away from her family and friends, when Jesus was a baby. That is strong. She followed Jesus to the cross and stood by him, even though it hurt her to see him die. That is strong. She kept her faith and followed what God asked of her, even when she did not understand. She was meek.

In your life, meekness might look a little different. For example, sometimes when a younger brother or sister takes a toy you were using, you might want to snatch it back and yell or hit. And since you are bigger, stronger, and faster, you could do that. But should you? No. If you are practicing being meek like Mary, you would take a deep breath, say a quick prayer asking for help, and calmly use your words to ask for your toy back.

This takes lots of practice and hard work. But you are strong. You are capable. It's important to learn to use your strength well and be meek like Mary.

Conversation Starters _____

- How can you show meekness like Mary?

- When do you need help with meekness? How can I help you practice it?

Day Thirteen

Obedience

Obedience is hard. Sometimes we have our own ideas about what we want to do or where we want to go. Sometimes we want to do things our way. And there are times when we will get our own way, times when we can do what we want. But we do have to listen to our parents, and we always need to listen to God. Mary always obeyed God. She knew that he loved her. She knew that he wanted what was best for her and for all his children (us included), and that must mean that his way was going to be the best way.

Just like he did with Adam and Eve, God gave us free will. That means we get to decide if we are going to follow him or not. Every day we get to choose our behaviors. Everyday we have a new chance to choose to do what is good and right. Mary always said yes to God; she always chose what was good and right. It's importance to practice obedience, to trust that God, and your mom and dad, want good things for you.

Conversation Starters

- When are some times you've obeyed your parents? When have you disobeyed them?
- How do you feel when you are asked to obey? Why do you think you feel that way?

- How do you feel after you obey? How do you feel after you disobey?
- What helps you to obey? What makes it hard?

Day Fourteen

Faith

Faith means to believe in God and all that he has revealed. It is incredibly important. Faith helps us to trust God, to know him, and to love him. Faith is many things, but it is not boring. When you have faith in God, you get to be a part of his big story.

God has many adventures planned for you, and wonderful people and experiences he wants to bring into your life. He knew you before he created you, he loved you before you were born. When we have faith we can say confidently, "Jesus, I trust in you" no matter what is happening.

Mary had faith. She knew that Jesus was God, and so she wasn't afraid when she stood next to him on the cross. She knew that he had said he would rise again, and she trusted him. God led Mary on a great adventure, and because she always believed in him no matter what, she is now Queen of Heaven and sits joyfully with him there.

Conversation Starters

- Can you think of any other people that God led on a great adventure?

- What kind of adventure do you think he has in store for you?

Day Fifteen

Humility

Humility means that you know who you are. You know your own worth and value as a child of God. When we are humble, we are confident that God made us and loves us, and we don't try to be someone that we aren't. Everyone has gifts and talents, and everyone has things that are hard for them.

Mary is a wonderful example of humility. When Mary met Elizabeth, and Elizabeth recognized her as the mother of the Savior, Mary joyfully thanked God for the gifts he has given her. She never tried to hide the gift of being Jesus' mom, but she always thanked God for the amazing blessing of being the Mother of God.

Some children learn to read very easily, but for others it takes a lot of work. Some kids are very good at climbing trees or playing sports, but others aren't good at it right away. Some kids find it easy to obey, and some don't. Some kids have a hard time not getting angry when they don't get what they want.

When we are humble, we understand the things that we are good at as well as the things that are hard for us. We learn to take all of them to Jesus. When we give our gifts to Jesus and use them to do what he wants, he makes them even better, and when we give him our struggles, he helps us overcome them.

Conversation Starters

- What are some things that you are good at?
- What are some things that are hard for you to do?

- How do you feel when you see another kid doing easily what is difficult for you? How do you think Jesus wants you to feel?

Day Sixteen

How to Love God with Your Whole Heart

God loves you so much. He loves you widely, and deeply, and truly. He loves you even more than your mom and dad do. He is the best friend you will ever have, the person who knows you best, the one who won't ever let you down. Getting to know God and being his friend is a wonderful thing. Mary learned to love God with her whole heart. She fell in love with God. You can trust him to love you no matter what. The more you get to know Jesus, the easier it is to love him and trust him. It's hard to love people we don't know. The way that we get to know Jesus may look a little different than the ways that you get to know your friends, but it is still possible. We can read his words in the Bible, we can look at his picture, we can listen to stories about his life. These are all ways that will help us know Jesus and love him.

When we love God with our whole heart and allow ourselves to be filled with his love, we choose him and his way above other things. We learn to want what God wants and are happy.

Conversation Starters

- Who is your best friend? Why is she your best friend? How did you get to know her? What kinds of things do you like to do together?
- Do you think you could get to know Jesus in the same way?

What are some ways to get to know Jesus?
- Today's illustration shows Mary as a queen offering her heart to God. What do you notice about this picture? What do you think she's feeling?

Day Seventeen

Prayer for Help

Yesterday we talked about how to love God with your whole heart. Today, let's learn a prayer that will help us to do that. This is a great prayer to learn by heart and say every day. Maybe we can make it part of our morning routine and say it together. As we pray it, think about what it means and what we are asking Mary to help us with.

> Holy Mary,
> Obtain for me the help I need,
> to do my very best
> using all the powers within me
> and all the talents and skills I possess,
> according to my possibilities,
> to fulfill God's plan
> in every circumstance of my life. Amen.

Conversation Starters _____

- Are there any words in this prayer that you didn't understand? Can I say it in an easier way for you?

- What do you need help from God with today?

Day Eighteen

The Annunciation

For the next few days, we are going to focus on what the Scriptures tell us about Mary's life.

LUKE 1:26–38

In the sixth month the angel Gabriel was sent from God to a city of Galilee named Nazareth, to a virgin betrothed to a man whose name was Joseph, of the house of David; and the virgin's name was Mary. And he came to her and said, "Hail, full of grace, the Lord is with you!" But she was greatly troubled at the saying, and considered in her mind what sort of greeting this might be. And the angel said to her, "Do not be afraid, Mary, for you have found favor with God. And behold, you will conceive in your womb and bear a son, and you shall call his name Jesus.

> He will be great, and will be called the Son of the Most High;
> and the Lord God will give to him the throne of his father David,
> and he will reign over the house of Jacob for ever;
> and of his kingdom there will be no end."

And Mary said to the angel, "How shall this be, since I have no husband?" And the angel said to her,

> "The Holy Spirit will come upon you,
> and the power of the Most High will overshadow you;
> therefore the child to be born will be called holy,
> the Son of God.

And behold, your kinswoman Elizabeth in her old age has also conceived a son; and this is the sixth month with her who was called barren. For with God nothing will be impossible." And Mary said, "Behold, I am the handmaid of the Lord; let it be to me according to your word." And the angel departed from her.

Day Nineteen

The Visitation

LUKE 1:39–56

In those days Mary arose and went with haste into the hill country, to a city of Judah, and she entered the house of Zechariah and greeted Elizabeth. And when Elizabeth heard the greeting of Mary, the child leaped in her womb; and Elizabeth was filled with the Holy Spirit and she exclaimed with a loud cry, "Blessed are you among women, and blessed is the fruit of your womb! And why is this granted me, that the mother of my Lord should come to me? For behold, when the voice of your greeting came to my ears, the child in my womb leaped for joy. And blessed is she who believed that there would be a fulfilment of what was spoken to her from the Lord." And Mary said,

> "My soul magnifies the Lord, and my spirit rejoices in God my Savior, for he has regarded the low estate of his handmaiden. For behold, henceforth all generations will call me blessed; for he who is mighty has done great things for me, and holy is his name. And his mercy is on those who fear him from generation to generation. He has shown strength with his arm, he has scattered the proud in the imagination of their hearts, he has put down the mighty from their thrones, and exalted those of low degree; he has filled the hungry with good things, and the rich he has sent empty away. He has helped his servant Israel, in remembrance of his mercy, as he spoke to our fathers, to Abraham and to his posterity for ever."

And Mary remained with her about three months, and returned to her home.

Day Twenty

The Birth of Jesus

LUKE 2:1–14

In those days a decree went out from Caesar Augustus that all the world should be enrolled. This was the first enrollment, when Quirinius was governor of Syria. And all went to be enrolled, each to his own city. And Joseph also went up from Galilee, from the city of Nazareth, to Judea, to the city of David, which is called Bethlehem, because he was of the house and lineage of David, to be enrolled with Mary, his betrothed who was with child. And while they were there, the time came for her to be delivered. And she gave birth to her first-born son and wrapped him in swaddling cloths, and laid him in a manger, because there was no place for them in the inn.

And in that region there were shepherds out in the field, keeping watch over their flock by night. And an angel of the Lord appeared to them, and the glory of the Lord shone around them, and they were filled with fear. And the angel said to them, "Be not afraid; for behold, I bring you good news of a great joy which will come to all the people; for to you is born this day in the city of David a Savior, who is Christ the Lord. And this will be a sign for you: you will find a baby wrapped in swaddling cloths and lying in a manger." And suddenly there was with the angel a multitude of the heavenly host praising God and saying, "Glory to God in the highest, and on earth peace among men with whom he is pleased!"

Day Twenty-One

The Visit of the Shepherds

LUKE 2:15–18

When the angels went away from them into heaven, the shepherds said to one another, "Let us go over to Bethlehem and see this thing that has happened, which the Lord has made known to us." And they went with haste, and found Mary and Joseph, and the baby lying in a manger. And when they saw it they made known the saying which had been told them concerning this child; and all who heard it wondered at what the shepherds told them.

The Presentation in the Temple

LUKE 2:22, 25–35

And when the time came for their purification according to the law of Moses, they brought him up to Jerusalem to present him to the Lord. ... Now there was a man in Jerusalem, whose name was Simeon, and this man was righteous and devout, looking for the consolation of Israel, and the Holy Spirit was upon him. And it had been revealed to him by the Holy Spirit that he should not see death before he had seen the Lord's Christ. And inspired by the Spirit he came into the temple; and when the parents brought in the child Jesus, to do for him according to the custom of the law, he took him up in his arms and blessed God and said,

> "Lord, now let your servant depart in peace,
> according to your word;
> for my eyes have seen your salvation
> which you have prepared in the presence of all peoples,
> a light for revelation to the Gentiles,
> and for glory to your people Israel."

And his father and his mother marveled at what was said about him; and Simeon blessed them and said to Mary his mother,

> "Behold, this child is set for the fall and rising of many in Israel,
> and for a sign that is spoken against
> (and a sword will pierce through your own soul also),
> that thoughts out of many hearts may be revealed."

Day Twenty-Three

Finding Jesus in the Temple

LUKE 2:41–52

Now his parents went to Jerusalem every year at the feast of the Passover. And when he was twelve years old, they went up according to custom; and when the feast was ended, as they were returning, the boy Jesus stayed behind in Jerusalem. His parents did not know it, but supposing him to be in the company they went a day's journey, and they sought him among their kinsfolk and acquaintances; and when they did not find him, they returned to Jerusalem, seeking him. After three days they found him in the temple, sitting among the teachers, listening to them and asking them questions; and all who heard him were amazed at his understanding and his answers. And when they saw him they were astonished; and his mother said to him, "Son, why have you treated us so? Behold, your father and I have been looking for you anxiously." And he said to them, "How is it that you sought me? Did you not know that I must be in my Father's house?" And they did not understand the saying which he spoke to them. And he went down with them and came to Nazareth, and was obedient to them; and his mother kept all these things in her heart. And Jesus increased in wisdom and in stature, and in favor with God and man.

Day Twenty-Four

The Wedding at Cana

JOHN 2:1–12

On the third day there was a marriage at Cana in Galilee, and the mother of Jesus was there; Jesus also was invited to the marriage, with his disciples. When the wine failed, the mother of Jesus said to him, "They have no wine." And Jesus said to her, "O woman, what have you to do with me? My hour has not yet come." His mother said to the servants, "Do whatever he tells you." Now six stone jars were standing there, for the Jewish rites of purification, each holding twenty or thirty gallons. Jesus said to them, "Fill the jars with water." And they filled them up to the brim. He said to them, "Now draw some out, and take it to the steward of the feast." So they took it. When the steward of the feast tasted the water now become wine, and did not know where it came from (though the servants who had drawn the water knew), the steward of the feast called the bridegroom and said to him, "Every man serves the good wine first; and when men have drunk freely, then the poor wine; but you have kept the good wine until now." This, the first of his signs, Jesus did at Cana in Galilee, and manifested his glory; and his disciples believed in him.

After this he went down to Capernaum, with his mother and his brothers and his disciples; and there they stayed for a few days.

Day Twenty-Five

Mary at the Crucifixion

JOHN 19:25–27

But standing by the cross of Jesus were his mother, and his mother's sister, Mary the wife of Clopas, and Mary Magdalene. When Jesus saw his mother, and the disciple whom he loved standing near, he said to his mother, "Woman, behold, your son!" Then he said to the disciple, "Behold, your mother!" And from that hour the disciple took her to his own home.

Day Twenty-Six

Our Lady and the Miraculous Medal

Sometimes Mary has a specific message that she wants to share with the world, or with a certain place or certain people. When she does, she will appear to a person, often a child, and talk to them. When Mary appears to someone, we call it a Marian *apparition*. We call the people who have seen and spoken to Mary *seers*.

Over the next few days, we are going to learn about some Marian apparitions. Pay attention to what happened, how the seers felt, and what Mary said. Think about how you would have felt in their situations. What would you have said to Mary? How would you have felt?

• • •

Sister Catherine awoke suddenly in the middle of the night. Someone was calling her name. She looked around and saw a small child, surrounded by light. Somehow she knew — he was her guardian angel. She followed and he led her to the sisters' chapel. Sister Catherine marveled that all the candles in the chapel were lit, as though it was Christmas! She heard a soft rustling sound, the sound of silk in a lady's dress. She looked around and saw that there *was* a lady in the chapel! She was wearing a beautiful ivory dress, with a long blue mantle and a white veil. "Here is the Blessed Virgin," said Catherine's guardian angel. Mary sat down in the blue velvet chair used by the priest during Mass. Catherine knelt at her feet and rested her head on Mary's lap. Mary told her that God had a special mission for her (tomorrow we'll learn more about this mission.)

Conversation Starters

• What do you think Catherine thought when she saw her guardian angel?
• How do you think she felt when she put her head on Mary's lap? Why do you think she did that?

• What do you think you would have done if you were Catherine? Is there anything you would have asked Mary or wanted to talk about with her while you cuddled with her?

Day Twenty-Seven

Prayer of the Miraculous Medal

Yesterday we learned about the time when Mary appeared in Paris to Saint Catherine Labouré. Mary appeared to Saint Catherine three times. The second time Mary appeared, she was standing on top of a globe, with her feet crushing the head of a serpent. Then Catherine saw rays of light streaming from Mary's hands. Mary explained that these symbolized the graces that she pours out on the people who ask. Catherine saw this sentence around Mary: "O Mary, conceived without sin, pray for us who have recourse to thee." Mary asked Catherine to have a medal made with this sentence and the image on it. She promised that those who wear it with confidence would receive many graces.

Today let's practice a prayer that goes along with the Miraculous Medal. During this prayer, when we say the word *recourse*, we mean the way we take our trouble to Mary. This prayer asks Mary to remember all of the people who turn to her when they're in need and all of the people who don't. Listen:

> O Mary, conceived without sin, pray for us who have recourse to you, and for all who do not have recourse to you, especially the enemies of the Church and those recommended to you. Amen.

Conversation Starters

- Have you ever seen a Miraculous Medal?
- Do you know what the word *miraculous* means?

- Why do you think that we pray for the people who don't have recourse to Mary?

Day Twenty-Eight

Our Lady of Lourdes

One day, fourteen-year-old Bernadette Soubirous was out collecting firewood with her sister and friends. They crossed a river to find more, but Bernadette stayed behind. Suddenly, she saw a beautiful lady holding a rosary and with yellow roses at her feet. The lady was wearing a white robe and blue belt with a white veil and was surrounded by light and a golden cloud. She was smiling. Bernadette was scared and tried to make the Sign of the Cross over herself for protection, but she couldn't, not until the lady made the Sign of the Cross first. Then Bernadette prayed the Rosary. While she prayed, the lady's fingers moved over the beads. She said the Glory Be with Bernadette.

Bernadette did not know who the lady was, and no one believed her when she told them about what she had seen. But even so, Bernadette felt like she just had to go back to the little stone grotto (a *grotto* is a small cave) where she had seen her.

The lady (who of course was Mary) appeared to Bernadette eighteen times at the grotto. She asked Bernadette to pray for sinners and their conversion. Mary also gave a miraculous spring of water at the site, where many thousands of people have come and been healed of their illnesses.

Later, when Bernadette asked the lady her name, she replied, "I am the Immaculate Conception." Bernadette did not know what this meant, but she told her pastor the name and that the lady wanted a chapel built at the grotto. Today Lourdes is a place where thousands and thousands of people go each year to ask Mary to pray for them and their families.

Conversation Starters

- How would you have felt if you were Bernadette and saw a mysterious lady? Who would you have told about it?

- Do you think you would have gone back to the grotto like Bernadette did?

Day Twenty-Nine

The Sign of the Cross

One of the most important things that Bernadette learned from Mary was how to make the Sign of the Cross correctly. Throughout her life, Bernadette always told people that it was important to make the Sign of the Cross well, and she was right. The Sign of the Cross should always be made reverently. That means we should make it with respect for God. For many people, this prayer is the first thing they do in the morning, and the last thing they do before they go to sleep. What a wonderful way to start and end your day!

The proper way to make the Sign of the Cross is to use your right hand. First, touch your fingers to your forehead, saying, "In the name of the Father," then to your chest, saying, "and of the Son," then to your left shoulder, saying, "and of the Holy Spirit," and finally to your right shoulder, saying, "Amen."

We use this prayer so frequently that sometimes we can forget its significance and don't give it the attention it deserves. Sometimes we even forget that it's a prayer all on its own! When we make the Sign of the Cross, we are marking ourselves with the sign of Jesus' victory over death. This is a powerful blessing. It is a sign that we belong to Jesus!

Let's practice together making the Sign of the Cross over ourselves now, going slowly and thinking about God as we do.

Conversation Starters

- When have you noticed people making the Sign of the Cross? Why do you think that people make it then?

- Now that we've learned a little more about it, are there times during your day that you would like to start praying the Sign of the Cross?

Day Thirty

Our Lady of Fátima

Lucia, who was nine years old, and her cousins, Francisco (who was eight) and Jacinta (who was six), were tending their sheep in the countryside in Portugal. They had just finished praying a Rosary when they saw a beautiful woman in white hovering above a tree. She told them not to be afraid.

Our Lady appeared to the three children six times. She asked them to pray the Rosary daily for sinners, and explained that she wanted the whole world consecrated to her. The children were also given a very scary vision of hell, and they understood the need to keep praying for the conversion of souls (that is, for people to turn their hearts back to Jesus).

Our Lady promised she would send a miracle on the day of the last apparition, October 13, 1917, so that all of the people who thought the children were lying about seeing Mary would come to believe. That morning, thousands of people gathered in the field of the apparitions and waited.

Lucia, Francisco, and Jacinta saw Mary arrive. Mary asked them to have a chapel built in her honor, and told them that she was the Lady of the Rosary. Mary reminded them to pray for sinners, and that people needed to change their ways and not offend God. Then Mary disappeared, and the children saw Saint Joseph holding the Child Jesus. Saint Joseph and Jesus blessed the crowd. Then Mary and Jesus appeared again, and Jesus blessed the crowd again.

While the children were seeing this, the people in the field saw something very different. They witnessed the Miracle of the Sun. Suddenly, up in the sky, the sun began to twirl and dance about! Nothing like it had ever been seen before.

Conversation Starters

- How do you think you would have felt if you were Lucia, Jacinta, or Francisco the first time you saw Mary? What about the second time? Would you have been excited that she came back?
- What do you think it would be like to see the sun dance?

Day Thirty-One

Prayers of Fátima

Yesterday we learned about the apparition of Mary at Fátima. Over the course of the apparitions, the children were given two wonderful prayers to pray for the church, one by Mary, and one by an angel who also appeared to them. They are short prayers that we can say every day, whenever we remember, and whenever we feel called to pray for sinners.

O my Jesus, forgive us our sins, save us from the fires of hell. Lead all souls to heaven, especially those in most need of your mercy. Amen.

My God, I believe, I adore, I hope, and I love you! I beg pardon of those who do not believe, do not adore, do not hope, and do not love you. Amen.

Conversation Starters

- Are there any words in these prayers that you don't understand? Can I explain them to you?

- Why do you think it's important to pray for sinners?

Day Thirty-Two

The Litany of Loreto

On this last day of our preparation period, we are going to say part of a very special prayer together. It's called a litany. A litany is a prayer that looks like a list, but one person begins and another responds. I'll say the beginning, and you'll say the response after me. It's easy! Pay attention to all of the wonderful names for Mary in this litany. We give Mary nicknames just like we do our family and friends. These special names show her how much we love her. Afterwards, we can talk about our favorite ones, or any that confused you or that you didn't understand. If you have a question in the middle, that's okay too. We can always pause for an explanation.

Holy Mary, pray for us.
Holy Mother of God, …
Holy Virgin of Virgins,
Mother of Christ,
Mother of divine grace,
Mother most pure,
Mother of good counsel,
Mother of our Creator,
Mother of our Savior,
Virgin most prudent,

Virgin most venerable,
Virgin most renowned,
Virgin most powerful,
Virgin most merciful,
Virgin most faithful,
Mirror of justice,
Seat of wisdom,
Cause of our joy,
Spiritual vessel,
Vessel of honor,

Singular vessel of devotion,
Mystical rose,
Tower of David,
Tower of ivory,
House of gold,
Ark of the covenant,
Gate of heaven,
Morning star,
Health of the sick,
Refuge of sinners,

Comforter of the afflicted,
Help of Christians,
Queen of Angels,
Queen of all Saints,
Queen of the most
   holy Rosary,
Queen of families,
Queen of peace, pray for us.

Conversation Starters

- This prayer is full of different names for Mary. What are your favorites?

- What questions do you have about any of the names of Mary?

Day Thirty-Three

Consecration Day

Hooray! We have arrived! Today we will make our consecration to Mary. When we go to Mass today, we will say a very special prayer after Communion. We will kneel and whisper the words quietly together, giving our hearts, bodies, and souls into her care, and knowing that she will bring us to Jesus.

A simple act of consecration:
My Jesus, I am all yours and all that I have is yours, through Mary, your Holy Mother.

For Parents

Who Is Mary?

Day One — Mary Was a Little Girl Once

Parents, this is a wonderful opportunity to help your child understand that Mary was a real person, rooted in history. I found that showing my daughter photos of the Holy Land while we talked was helpful in making Mary come alive to her. Maybe you or someone you know has been there, and walked where Mary walked. If so, take the time to tell your child about the trip, to share the experiences. Even if you haven't traveled to Israel, you can still find fabulous shots of Nazareth and Jerusalem on the internet. I love being able to take advantage of technology as a tool for learning! You can also take out a map of the world, to show your child where you live, and then follow your finger all the way to Israel. Many Bibles contain maps. My daughter Gianna loves looking at the maps in her children's Bible, to try and see where the stories happen.

This can also be a day when you both use your imaginations. I know Gianna has lots of ideas about what Mary was like as a little girl! Imagine Mary playing, running, skipping, jumping. Imagine what her house would have been like, what she would have liked to play, what chores she might have done to help her family.

Day Two — Mary Is the Immaculate Conception

The Catholic Church is rich in symbolism, and in today's illustration, Rebecca has included many symbols from the lineage and life of Jesus and hidden them behind Saint Anne and Mary. Many of the symbols you'll see are common in Jesse Tree devotions during Advent. The Jesse Tree is an activity where children place an ornament on the tree for each day of Advent. Each day they read a story from the Bible and learn a little bit more about salvation history. It tells the story of Jesus' lineage, of how God was moving and working in the world and in the Jewish people to prepare a way for his Son.

I love that the artist has interwoven the symbols into the tree, because it roots Saint Anne and Mary in the larger story of salvation. They are at the center, because Christ, the child that Mary will bear, is at the center, and because Mary, the Immaculate Conception, is the crown of creation, and her birth moves the story from the Old Testament to the New.

Today is a great day to play spot the hidden pictures and teach your child what they mean. In no particular order, here are the symbols hidden in the tree and their meanings:

Staff: This symbolizes Christ as the Good Shepherd. Bible passages to learn more about this symbol: John 10:7–18, Matthew 18:12–14, and Luke 15:3–7.

Lamp: This symbol comes from the first book of Samuel (1 Sm 3:1-18). This is the story of the Lord calling Samuel.

Moses basket: *Moses baskets* get their name from the Exodus story about the birth of Moses (Ex 2: 1–10). It tells the tale of how Moses was saved from the Nile River by Pharaoh's daughter.

Star of David: The six-pointed Star of David has long been a symbol of the Jewish people in general, and their great King David more specifically. The Bible passage for this symbol is 1 Samuel 16:1–13, and is the story of David's anointing as the future king of Israel.

Scales: The scales are a symbol for Solomon, and stand for his wisdom in judgment. The story is told in 1 Kings 3:5–14. God tells Solomon to ask for anything he wants, and Solomon, in humility, asks for wisdom.

Sun and moon: The sun and moon are symbols of creation, the story of which you'll find at the beginning of the Book of Genesis.

Sword: The sword is a symbol of the sword that would pierce Mary's heart, as foretold by Simeon in Luke 2:25–35.

Ladder: The ladder represents the promises God made to Jacob in Genesis 28:10–15.

Hammer: The hammer is a symbol of Saint Joseph, the earthly father of Jesus, a carpenter. When we talk about Mary, sometimes we can forget to remember that she had tremendous support from Saint Joseph, who was himself a righteous, holy man of God.

Ark: The ark is a symbol of the story of Noah, which is found in Genesis 6.

Bundle of wheat: The bundle of wheat is the symbol for Ruth, one of four women mentioned in the lineage of Jesus at the beginning of the Gospel of Matthew.

Day Three — Prayer to the Immaculate Conception

The Immaculate Conception is one of the most misunderstood points of Catholic doctrine. When most people think of it, they think of Jesus being conceived in Mary's womb, and are often surprised to find that it refers to Mary's conception in the womb of Saint Anne. If you're looking for more on this doctrine, you can read the apostolic constitution, *Ineffabilis Deus,* by Pope Pius IX.

Day Four — Mary Is the Mother of God

Theotokos — pronounced *thay-oh-TOH-kohs*

Parents, Mary as mother will be a natural connection for your children. A mother is something that kids understand, have an image of, and experience of. By encouraging your children to imagine Mary and Jesus as mother and child you are helping bring to life for them an important role that Mary will play in their own lives.

Day Five — Mary Is Our Mom Too

Parents, this is a great day to share your experiences of Mary as a mother with your children. When have you felt her love in your life? Why did you consecrate your life to her? What things do you as an adult ask Mary for help with? In our home, we've found that getting into the habit of praying out loud has been very helpful in showing our children how to relate to God and to Mary. It can be awkward at first, but it has been very fruitful for our children to see that we talk to Mary throughout the day, and that they can approach her with things big and small.

If you're new to Marian devotion, this is a great day to share a little bit with your child about what drew you to Mary. I know for me, I first started really building a relationship with her when I started noticing her "showing up" in my prayer time. It seemed like every time I opened the Bible, read something from a saint, or did any kind of spiritual reading, there she was. It felt like she was trying to get my attention, so I stopped and listened.

It's hard to share these intimate moments of our spiritual lives with our children, but it is so important for their own spiritual growth. Even if what you're sharing with them is that you felt a call, or were drawn to her without knowing why, it's valuable for your child to see you as a person who pays attention when she prays and is willing to follow even when she doesn't understand everything.

Day Six — The Memorare

Memorare — pronounced *Meh-moh-RAH-ray*

Parents, this is a great place to talk to your child about the way that God can speak to us through the words of rote prayers. Think about what words stuck out to you when you prayed the Memorare just now. Share with your child a little about the word and why it moved your heart. For example, I might point out the word *gracious*, and explain that I love thinking about Mary as an example of what it means to be gracious when someone asks for help — she's not grouchy with me, no matter how many times

I come to her.

Day Seven — Mary Is Filled with the Holy Spirit

Parents, this is a great day to share the times in your lives when you have felt the Holy Spirit moving in your life. Have you ever felt the Holy Spirit urging you to do something? To say something? What did it feel like? How did you know it was the Holy Spirit? Here's an example of a story about the Holy Spirit that I shared with my daughter.

> A long time ago, when I was still living in Georgia, I had the opportunity to move to Michigan. It didn't make a lot of sense to me — Aunt Caitlin and Alexander were in Georgia, and I loved it there. But, I felt in my heart that moving was what the Holy Spirit was asking me to do. I knew it was the Holy Spirit because I had been speaking with him in my prayers for many years and could recognize his voice, just like I recognize yours when we talk. When a thought comes into my head that is from the Holy Spirit, my heart starts to beat fast and hard, boom, boom, boom. And the thought doesn't go away. It happened like that when God asked me to move to Michigan. And you know what happened when I came here? I met your daddy, and then we got married and had you. I'm so glad I listened to the voice of the Holy Spirit, because daddy lived in Michigan, and I wouldn't have met him otherwise.

You'll notice that this story is simple. As an adult, I'm sure you can guess that there are many more details about my discernment and the events leading up to and after such a big move. And as my children get older, and we have more discussions about what it means to listen to the voice of God in their lives, we will revisit this story in more depth. But for now, with my very young daughter, this simplistic version of the story hit the points that I want to expose her to. First, that it is possible to hear the Holy Spirit speaking in her life. Second, that it takes cultivating a relationship to be able to recognize his voice well. Third, sometimes you don't understand what God is asking, and it's okay to feel confused or nervous. Finally, that listening to the Holy Spirit will lead to joy.

As you think about telling your story of experience with the Holy Spirit, remember to keep in mind what lessons you want your child to take away from the story. Also, remember to share some details about how you felt throughout the experience, and especially what the Holy Spirit sounds like to your heart.

Day Eight — Mary Is Queen of Heaven

Parents, heaven can be a tricky subject for little ones, especially because talking about heaven necessitates talking about death. In this, I always try to follow Maria Montessori's guideline of "follow the child." Depending on your child's level of curiosity, interest, and your comfort level, this conversation can be short and sweet, along the lines of "when we die, we go to heaven to be with Jesus and to be happy forever," or could involve a longer conversation of heaven, hell, and purgatory.

Our children, though young, have experienced the death of a loved one. Gianna's earliest memory is actually her great-grandmother's funeral. William was too young to remember that, but does remember fondly our elderly neighbor, Mr. Jim, who passed away last year. William is quite content to know that when people are good, they die and go to heaven and are happy. He prays for Mr. Jim, and is happy that he is with Mary and Jesus. He has not asked the questions that would cause a longer explanation and is not ready for one. Gianna, on the other hand, had many questions about death, and I found myself having rather in-depth conversations with a three-year-old about burial, decomposition, what hell is, how purgatory works, and what heaven is like.

My husband and I agreed that we would not shy away from honest answers about tough subjects, but do believe in giving children the amount of truth they are capable of receiving. So as you talk with your child, I encourage you to follow their lead. What questions are they asking? What details are they picking out and focusing on? Let them be the guides of this conversation, and answer their questions as simply and as clearly as you are able.

Day Nine — Mary Always Leads Us to Jesus

Parents, the inspiration for today's illustration comes from Our Lady of Czestochowa, an icon in Poland. Her crown says the words *Totus Tuus*, meaning "All Yours," which is a quote from Saint Louis de Montfort and the papal motto of Saint John Paul II, who was also Polish.

What Can We Learn from Mary?

Day Ten — How to Say Yes to God

Trusting in God's plan without always understanding it is one of the most difficult aspects of our walk of faith. As a parent, I am reminded constantly of what a good job Saints Anne and Joachim did with Mary in preparing her to say yes to being the mother of Jesus. Certainly they didn't know what God was going to ask of their daughter, but they knew, just as we know, that God had a plan for their daughter's life. And they also must have known that it's hard to trust a Person we don't know. They spent their daughter's childhood teaching her who God was, teaching her and showing her that he loved her, that he wanted what was best for her, so that when God asked big things of their daughter, she didn't hesitate.

This is what I want for my own children. I don't know that I'll do as good a job as Saint Anne and Saint Joachim, but I'm going to give my all to making sure that my children know the Lord as a loving Father who has their best interests at heart.

Day Eleven — How to Be in the Presence of God

Parents, this is a great day to share the ways you practice the presence of God throughout your day. What pockets of time do you find for prayer? How can you help your children find them too?

For example, in our family, we say a quick thank you prayer when we pull into our driveway each time, to remember that God got us safely home. I've also found that alarms on my phone help me to remember to stop and pray. My kids have gotten to recognize the bells of the alarm and stop to pray themselves.

If you want to do more to pray throughout the day, think of some ways you can do that either alone or with your spouse and family.

Day Twelve — Meekness

Meekness is a concept that is widely misunderstood. I grew up with the idea that someone who was meek was mild-mannered and weak, someone who didn't feel things strongly, the personification of pastel colors, if that makes sense. It was a word with negative connotations for me. It took a long time for me to change my own mindset, to allow the true definition of meekness, that is, strength under control, to seep into my worldview. As I teach my daughter about Mary, as we look to her as our example of this virtue, we spend time focusing on her strength, her giftedness, her power.

At Calvary, we know she felt her grief strongly. And yet, when we see her depicted along the way of the cross, or at the foot of the cross, she is strong, unmoving, the opposite of Mary Magdalene, whose grief overcame her. Mary knew she had more to do. She stood as a consolation to her Son, by his side until the end, and took his people as her own, becoming their mother in spirit and truth. That is the picture that I want in my daughter's head as she learns about meekness.

Day Thirteen — Obedience

Obedience is hard, even for us adults. Sometimes kids don't realize it. They're used to seeing us as the people who they have to obey, not as people who have to obey themselves. I know that my own children respond when my husband and I share with them our own struggles with obedience.

As Catholics we are asked for a lot of obedience — to our bishops, to our pope, to Church doctrine. We might not always understand the decisions that are made by Church authorities or the many facets of the various doctrines of the Church.

Day Fourteen — Faith

Parents, this is a wonderful day to share a little of the adventure God has led you on. Are there any parts of your love story with God that you can share with your child?

Day Fifteen — Humility

This, parents, is a difficult question for many of us to answer, but an incredibly important one for our children to know the answer to. By helping them to understand their own gifts, as well as their own areas of weakness, we can help them to understand what God's plan is for their lives. We can help them to understand that God knows them and loves all of them.

You can also share your own talents and gifts, along with areas that are a struggle for you. For example, I might share with Gianna that I have a talent for teaching, but I struggle with being patient when I'm tired, and that's hard for me as a mom and makes it difficult for me to teach her well. Then I would tell her how I bring that fatigue to Jesus and his mom, asking for extra grace during the day. I try to make sure that I stop and say a prayer when I am feeling frustrated or when I don't think I have enough patience.

Another avenue to pursue when talking about humility is to point out Saint Joseph in the illustration. Saint Joseph was a man, just like us, and he was the only member of the Holy Family who sinned. And yet, he knew who he was and was strong in his identity. He was asked to be the foster father of Jesus, the Savior, and he didn't shy away from that. He raised Jesus and was a dad to him, which took tremendous courage and humility.

Day Sixteen — How to Love God with Your Whole Heart

Today's conversation starters are about friendships, asking your kids how they interact with their best friends and how they got to know them. This is a great day to share a little bit about how you became friends with Jesus, how you got to know him. For example, I might share a story like this:

> When mommy was in college, before she met your daddy and had you, the Catholic Center I went to (where I met your Aunt Caitlin) had a little chapel. It was tiny, not bigger than our sunroom, and it had the most beautiful, colorful stained glass windows. It was cozy, and on Wednesdays, I would go after my classes finished and there would be adoration. The chapel was so little, that I could sit right next to the monstrance! I would tell Jesus all about my day, all about my classes, and all about the things I had planned with my friends. I would read from my Bible or from a book Miss Linda had given me about Jesus or Mary, and I would think about what I was reading. The more time I spent in the little chapel next to Jesus, the more I realized that I could hear him talking back to me in my heart, and the more I could feel him really there next to me in the Eucharist. I learned to be friends with Jesus by spending time with him.

You'll notice that my story is simple, and that I also included touch points for my kids — a reference to the time "before I met daddy," and mentions by name of people that they know, in this case their Aunt Caitlin and Miss Linda. Even though they cannot picture the chapel in their heads, as it's been years since we've been there, they can picture the people. Details like this make the story concrete for them. By adding details to your story you're reinforcing the reality of it to your child, moving it from a vague, generic tale, to something much more real. You're also building a foundation of witnessing your faith that you will be able to add to later.

Day Seventeen — Prayer for Help

I love today's illustration. Jesus and Mary doing laundry. What a simple and profound vision of the domestic church. For me, seeing Mary complete tasks for the sake of her family, like laundry, helps me to remember that she will step in and help me in the same way — cheerfully, gladly, and with her whole self.

Important Moments in Mary's Life: An Introduction to *Lectio Divina*

We are going to spend the next eight days meditating on important moments in the life of Mary using an ancient form of prayer called *lectio divina*. It is important to let Scripture speak to our children in its own words, because as Saint Ambrose said of the Lord, "we speak to him when we pray, we hear him when we read the Divine Oracles [Sacred Scripture]."

Pope Benedict XVI wrote in recommendation of the practice of *lectio divina* that, "the diligent reading of Sacred Scripture accompanied by prayer brings about that intimate dialogue in which the person reading hears God who is speaking, and in praying, responds to him with trusting openness of heart (cf. *Dei Verbum*, n. 25). If it is effectively promoted, this practice will bring to the Church — I am convinced of it — a new spiritual springtime." If we are to help renew our Church, and usher in this new spiritual springtime, we must introduce our children to all the riches the Church has to offer.

A simple version of *lectio divina* is appropriate and possible, even with a small child. Don't be discouraged by interruptions or distractions. Let your children be themselves while doing what you can to maintain a peaceful, positive experience with Scripture.

The full passage for lectio is included in the book for ease of use, but I do recommend taking out your personal Bible during this section of the consecration preparation. Maria Montessori, a Catholic herself, wrote in her book *The Absorbent Mind* that, "the senses, being explorers of the world, open the way to knowledge. Our apparatus for educating the senses offers child a key to guide his explorations of the world, they cast a light upon it which makes visible to him more things in greater detail than he could see in the dark, or uneducated state." For this reason, it's helpful to let children feel and experience the weight of the Bible, the importance of Sacred Scripture that can be transmitted through touching it. Let your children connect physically with God's word as you root them deeply in it.

When I sat down for the first time with our eldest, we climbed into the big bed in our room, I pulled her in close, and held the Bible between us. Reverently and quietly, I started to speak. I told her that this Bible was one of my most precious possessions, that I had owned it for even longer than I had known her daddy (truthfully, I've had my Bible since I was a college student, *much* longer than I've known her dad, but the period before mom met dad remains a mysterious and long ago time to our littles).

I opened the volume and started leafing through pages. My Bible is marked with highlights and underlining in many different colors, each corresponding to a different period and moment in my prayer life. I explained that while we don't usually write in books, the Bible is a little different, and that it's okay to underline or highlight a passage when you feel that God is speaking to you. I read to her some of the underlined passages, particularly choosing easy-to-understand chunks. I showed her the table of contents in the Bible, explaining that it is one book made up of many books, written by many people who listened to God. I showed her the notes from friends tucked carefully inside, the flowers pressed between the pages of the twelfth chapter of Wisdom that remind me of my day spent in prayer in the Mexican desert a decade ago.

In doing this, I was not attempting to school her in the use of the Bible — she can barely read, after all — but I was trying to make an impression on her heart. In slowly and reverently opening my Bible for her, I am modeling Christ, who opened the Scriptures to his disciples on the road to Emmaus. I am opening a new world to her, the world of God's word, where God speaks. I am showing her by my actions that this book matters, is special, is important; that this is not just another book on our shelf. Now, Gianna notices when the Bible comes out because she recognizes it. Sharing the Bible with her calls me deeper and continues to challenge me to model reverence and love of God's word.

If you have a Bible that you use in your own prayer life, or a special family Bible that has been passed down, I encourage you to use that one to explore with your child. Allow her to touch the delicate pages, slow down and create an air of importance. Make your voice a whisper, speak softly and gently. Caress the pages with your hand.

Note: There are no conversation starters for this section because they are built into the *lectio divina* process.

LECTIO METHOD FOR YOUNG CHILDREN
Before You Begin
Allow your children to snuggle in on your lap, bringing out your Bible to read to them. Show them your Bible, let them hold it, and feel the weight of the Word of God. Handle it with care, slowly turning the pages, mentioning special or favorite parts. In doing this, you will make Scripture more accessible to them. Express to them the wonder and joy we find in God's words in the way you touch the pages, in the way that you read the words.

Reading
Explain that you're going to read a passage from the Bible about Mary, and ask them to pay attention to what God is doing in the story and how Mary responds to the events in her life. Read the Scripture passage slowly, stopping to explain any new or unusual words.

Meditation
Ask if your children have any questions or comments about the story. Are they wondering about anything? Can they connect this story to other parts of the Bible they've heard? Does it remind them of anything in their own lives? If they don't have any questions, tell them what stood out for you in the story, what your favorite part was, or what you wonder about. You can also ask

some prompting questions, like "What's happening in the story?" "How were the characters feeling?" "How would you feel if you were _____?"

Prayer

Invite your children to respond to the story in prayer. Remind them that God gives us Scripture to teach us and help us to grow closer to him. Say something like, "Let's pray together about this story." Ask them what they would like to say to God about it. Be sure to model prayer for your child, praying out loud your response to the passage. You can thank God for the gift of Scripture, ask for help or insights, and speak about how it touched your heart. Help make the time prayerful for you both. Be gentle, calm, and snuggly.

Listening

This is the time for contemplation, which you can explain to your children as listening to God. Now that we've spoken to God, it's important to stop, quiet our hearts and minds, and listen for his response. Allow at least thirty seconds of quiet, explaining that we can listen to what God is saying in our hearts. If you child is restless, still try to model silence and peace during this time.

Closing

Ask if your children heard God speaking to their hearts. If not, reassure them that it's okay, that sometimes we are still learning how to listen for his voice, and sometimes he just likes to spend a quiet moment with us. Share some of how God spoke to your heart with your children. End by giving your children a blessing. One way to give a simple blessing is to place your hands on your children's heads and asking God (out loud) to bless them in the Name of Jesus and be with them throughout their day.

Marian Apparitions

With each of the apparitions, it's an opportunity to share in your child's wonder at the story, and also to share any connections with your child that you might have to the particular apparition. Do you perhaps have a devotion to Our Lady of Lourdes? Have you always wanted to visit Fátima? What didn't you know about the story? What questions do you have? What would you like to learn more about? Sharing what stands out to you about the particular apparition is another good way to connect.

Day Twenty-Six —Our Lady and the Miraculous Medal

What always strikes me about this apparition is that Mary appeared and then went to sit down in a chair, allowing Saint Catherine to lay her head on her lap while they talked. Isn't that just like a mom? I think that it makes this apparition the most accessible to young children, and it's a good day to get them using their imaginations and putting themselves in Catherine's position. I always share with my kids how much I wish I could lay my head on Mary's lap and tell her all my troubles.

Day Twenty-Seven — Prayer of the Miraculous Medal

Parents, this is a wonderful day to show your children a Miraculous Medal, if you happen to have one or wear one. (If not, you can easily find pictures online.) I have worn a Miraculous Medal since I was blessed enough to visit the little chapel of this apparition in college. My children are used to seeing it around my neck (except for when they have a baby sibling who might yank the chain), but on this day, I will unclasp the chain and let them see and hold it. I show them how the figure of Mary, raised on the medal, has been worn smooth, and explain that I often touch this medal when I am anxious or scared or upset because it reminds me of Mary and her protection, because it is a sacramental. A sacramental is an object that is blessed and helps the user connect more deeply to her faith. Other examples of sacramentals are Bibles and holy water. As physical objects that can be touched and used, sacramentals help engage our senses and order them towards the Lord.

Day Twenty-Eight — Our Lady of Lourdes

Bernadette Soubirous (pronounced SOO-bih-roo)
What strikes me about the Lourdes apparitions as an adult is Bernadette's reaction to them. A child of limited education, her response to the unexpected appearance of a lady in the grotto was to pray the Rosary. Isn't this what I want my children's reactions to the unexpected to be? Bernadette's first response to something surprising (and probably scary!) was to turn to Mary, by praying the Rosary. Teaching our children to turn to Mary is the whole point of this book, of this consecration preparation, and this apparition always reminds me why.

Day Twenty-Nine — The Sign of the Cross

Parents, the concept of the Trinity can be difficult to explain — three Persons in one God is a tricky concept for kids. Today's illustration can be of great help in showing children how the three Persons of the Trinity are related to one another.

Day Thirty — Our Lady of Fátima

The part of the story of Fátima that has always struck me, and seems more important than ever now that I'm a parent, is how faithful Lucia, Francisco, and Jacinta were, and how seriously they took the messages of the angel and Our Lady. Mary didn't shield them from the truth, and she didn't pull any punches about the importance of praying for and saving souls, the reality of hell, and the efficacy of prayer. I'm not suggesting that every child is ready for an in-depth discussion about eternal damnation, but this apparition is a good reminder to me as a mom of the capacity of my own children. I think sometimes we forget what our children can do, or at least I do. But when I do give them the opportunity to pray for a person in need, whether it be the sick neighbor, a homeless person on the side of the street, a family member having a hard time, or the souls buried in a graveyard as we pass by in the car, they always treat it with the utmost solemnity and sincerity. I need to remember to continue to offer my children more of these chances.

Day Thirty-One — Prayers of Fátima

These two prayers from the apparitions at Fátima are perfect for little ones to memorize because they are so short. We taught my eldest the "O My Jesus" prayer when she was three years old (she called it the "fires of hell" prayer for years, which always made me chuckle) and the other two as well, simply by adding it to our bedtime routine. Every night, before bed we say prayers with the kids. So when we want them to learn a new prayer, we just add it to the beginning or end of prayer time. Just by hearing it every day, the kids pick it up, usually in a span of a couple of weeks.

Day Thirty-Two — The Litany of Loreto

This is one of my very favorite litanies, and is a part of Saint Louis's consecration preparation. The names and titles of Mary are many, and so varied. I would encourage you, along with your children, to look up the history of any that you don't recognize or that you find yourself particularly drawn to. For me, my favorites are Mystical Rose and Health of the Sick.

Consecration Calendar

MARIAN FEAST DAY	DATE TO START	DATE OF CONSECRATION
Mary Mother of God	November 30	January 1
Our Lady of Lourdes	January 10	February 11
Annunciation	February 21	March 25
Our Lady of Fátima	April 11	May 13
Assumption	July 14	August 15
Mary's Birthday	August 7	September 8
Presentation of Mary	October 20	November 21
Our Lady of the Miraculous Medal	October 26	November 27
Immaculate Conception	November 6	December 8

Acknowledgments

This book would not exist without the encouragement and support of many people, the first of whom is my wonderful husband, who was the one to suggest that I should write a consecration for our family when I could not find one already in print and continued to urge me on as I dove deep into writing for the first time in a long time. My mother has been my biggest supporter throughout my life, and this endeavor was no different. Thank you, Mom, for all the babysitting you did and chores you pitched in on to make this book a reality. Thank you to Danielle and Kathryn, who prayed with me and for me through this whole process, and whose text message chain is a constant source of humor and consolation whenever I need it. Thank you to my wonderful father-in-law, Bill, who was my champion and read countless book proposal drafts, always offering just the right advice. To Mary Beth and Rebecca at OSV, I owe so much. Thank you both for your wisdom and guidance. And finally, this book would not be the same without the beautiful illustrations of Rebecca, who believed in this project enough to sign on when it was just a manuscript without a publisher.

About the Author

Colleen is a former missionary and Montessori teacher. She lives with her husband, grandmother, and children in Michigan, where she spends her time caring for Gram, homeschooling the children, and trying to find pockets of time to read. You can find more of Colleen's writing on her website, www.elevatortoheaven.com.

About the Artist

Originally from Virginia, Rebecca lives with her husband and children (including triplets) in Warsaw, Poland. When not frantically trying to keep the kids out of mischief, she enjoys reading, sewing, and music. She is currently on sabbatical from art and has returned to her dual career as scullery maid and pizza chef, having not cleaned the house for the entire year it took to finish the pictures for this book.